MASTERING THE BUCKET LIST

From Planning to Action

FORNEY SHELL

Forney Shell

Pan Piper Travel

Contents

SECTION ELEVEN

Dedication

To my wife, Judy, who put up with me as I learned the travel business. To my five sons, who are always encouraging. To Barbara, who provides continuing support, and to my clients, who are also my friends.

About the Author

Forney Shell is a travel agent who has supported clients in achieving their bucket list items for over eighteen years. A certified travel planner, Forney holds a Bachelor's degree in Business and a Master's degree in Human Resource Management. He began his career in aerospace engineering as a Senior Research Designer Engineer with Boeing aircraft and contributed his designs to the Apollo spacecraft and space shuttle. Forney is also a former professor of "Careers in Travel" at the College of Business and Technology in Charlottesville, Virginia.

forneyjr@embarqmail.com

Preface

I started my own bucket list when I was a teenager.

The first item on my list came from the movies I watched as a child. Back then, the "movies" included not only a movie but also a newsreel about national and international news events. Several years in a row, I watched with fascination as the newsreels featured an event known as the Grunion Run.

A grunion is a small fish that looks much like a sardine. Each year along the California coast, thousands of grunions come ashore to lay their eggs. The female grunion rides a wave to the beach, uses her tail to dig into the sand up to her gills, and lays the eggs. She must then ride one of the next three waves back to the ocean to survive. If she doesn't make it back in three waves, there is a great chance she will die on the beach.

Fascinated, I knew I wanted to see a Grunion Run for myself. It became the very first item on my bucket list. Many years later, my job took me to California, and I was finally able to see the Run for myself.

Since I knew I was in the right place to make this bucket list item happen, I tuned in to the local radio stations, waiting for their announcement that the timing was right for the Run.

From my research, I already knew I was in for a late-night outing to a deserted beach, but as with all Earth's creatures, nature has its own timeline. The first time I headed out to the beach, no grunions appeared. The second time, only four or five showed up. But the third time I ventured out, I saw thousands. And it was just as spectacular as I'd dreamed as a child.

The night was warm, the sky dark, and the sea was filled with plankton. Often when these small microorganisms are present, any motion in the water causes them to release a phosphorescent glow. That night, thanks to the active grunions swimming in the water, the sea was filled with hundreds of phosphorescent streaks. As I took in the moment, suddenly the grunion started coming ashore. I saw hundreds of grunions making their way out of the water at once, covering about twenty feet of shore. Two or three waves later, another several hundred came ashore twenty feet down the beach. Time seemed to slow as the show went for another hour, maybe more. After making their way out of the water, the females dug into the sand and laid their eggs. Then they flopped back on the sand for a few moments, obviously exhausted, before making the trip back to the sea, assuring their survival. It was an awe-inspiring sight, one I will never forget.

Another item on my bucket list also came about as the result of a movie. In my early twenties, I watched a movie based on the life of Rudolph Valentino. He was a famous silent film star who was especially well known for his mastery of the tango. In the film, Valentino showcased his tango skills. Immensely impressed by his ability, I decided if ever I had the chance to learn the tango, I would.

Many years later, my wife and I learned of an American Legion Post offering dance lessons. The dance they were teaching was the Foxtrot, not the tango, but we figured it would be fun, so we signed up. While we enjoyed learning, attendance was low, and at the third meeting, we were told they were cancelling the lessons. Knowing we were upset at the news, the instructor offered to teach us one more lesson, this time on any dance we wanted to learn. Remembering my long-ago dream, I jumped up and a requested a tango lesson.

Following that first lesson, I went on to learn many different tango steps. I'm not one to brag, but today I dance a pretty good tango. But it all began with a dream and a list. Thanks to my bucket list, I was able to do something new and amazing when the opportunity presented itself. With a strong bucket list, you, too, can embrace your life, your opportunities, and the world.

What is a Bucket List?

Life may be short, but it doesn't have to be uneventful. A bucket list is a list of things, places or people you want to meet, see, accomplish or experience in your lifetime. The purpose of this book is twofold: to help you develop your own bucket list, and to ensure you have a plan to accomplish the items on your list.

Throughout this book, I will share ideas and inspiration for creating a bucket list and discuss ways in which you may be able to accomplish them. Remember, a list must have at least two items and be written down (or typed up) to count as a list. Your list should be your own, but as you create it, I encourage you to think big and without restraint.

Most people only have vague ideas of things they want to do in the future floating around in the back of their minds. But you will never find "sometime" or "later" on any calendar. Because the desire is vague and the specifics feel remote, it is unlikely these fleeting thoughts will ever see the light of day.

Sitting down to create and write out an actual bucket list turns those ideas into something tangible. A physical list clarifies goals and opens the doors to accomplishment through intentional planning and execution. Your list can be read, reviewed frequently, updated and expanded. It can evolve as you evolve.

Many people have a fear of failure that keeps them from going after their dreams. The first step in overcoming that fear is writing out your list and reading it often. The very act of writing down your list will help overcome the fear of failure because you will have already succeeded with the first step.

Because the mind is an amazing thing, looking at your list, thinking about it often, and reading it aloud are extremely important. When you think about and recite the same thing repeatedly, the mind begins to perceive that thought as reality. This mental shift allows new ideas to start flowing. When you take action on these ideas, you begin to bring your dreams and goals to life.

By reading and applying the concepts in this book, it is my hope to guide you through the construction and eventual achievement of all the items on your list. If I can be of any help in developing your bucket list or planning your travel, please don't hesitate to contact me. Your bucket list success awaits!

SECTION ONE

NON-TRAVEL BUCKET LIST ITEMS

Non-Travel Bucket List Items

A GREAT MANY ITEMS ON A BUCKET LIST INVOLVE TRAVEL. FOR THAT reason, much of this book deals with travel and how it pertains to the items on your bucket list.

But there are also things on a bucket list unrelated to travel. These bucket list items may be material things, or they may be personal life achievements, such as:

1. Spending more time with your family
2. Getting in better physical shape
3. Developing a retirement plan
4. Obtaining a promotion at work or landing an ideal job

Though these bucket list items may seem very different than items on your list related to travel, the approach to achieving them is actually quite similar: It starts with a plan. Let's walk through the process for each of these common, non-travel, bucket list items.

Planning for Non-Travel Bucket List Items

No matter what you want to achieve, you must first write down your goals. Then, make a point to read them aloud at least twice a day, every day. This simple practice lays a foundation for success by embedding your focus firmly in your mind.

Next, it is time to plan. Remember, if you don't have a plan for success, you automatically have a plan for failure.

Spending More Time with Family

IF SPENDING MORE TIME WITH LOVED ONES IS ON YOUR LIST, DISCUSS your goal with your family. Determine what time is best for everyone to get together, and identify what everyone likes to do. Ask each other whether there are any existing activities or interests that can be turned into a family activity.

For example, if one family member plays a sport, can schedules be shifted so the whole family can participate, either on the team or as observers? Do multiple family members share a goal of getting in shape? An exercise plan for the whole family could provide more time together. Social and community groups always need volunteer workers; supporting a charitable organization might be another great way to bring your family together.

Once you've identified potential group activities, expand on your family time plan by answering the questions when, where, and how much. Are there tools or resources required for the activities you've selected? More information you need look up? Make your plan clear and specific so it matches your vision.

Getting in Better Physical Shape

NOW LET'S APPLY THE SAME PROCESS TO GETTING IN SHAPE - AN excellent example since we all struggle to stay motivated until we start to see results. Staying focused and motivated is what your written bucket list is all about. Each time you read it aloud (twice a day), you recommit to your goals.

Also, remember your version of success is your own. Just as spending time together as a family will differ among families, getting in shape does not have to mean going to the gym three times a week. It may mean nothing more than changing your diet. It could mean reading a book on working out at home or exercising along with a TV exercise program. If a program is not on at a time convenient for you, you can record it to watch later, perhaps with the whole family.

Once you've identified your preferred approach and activities, build out your plan. Are there books, videos or special equipment required? When will you get started? What costs are there to plan for? When getting in shape, remember it's a good idea to get a physical examination at the doctor's office first. Staying in shape also means taking preventative steps to stay healthy, including screenings like mammograms and prostate exams.

Developing a Retirement Plan

WHILE GETTING YOUR FINANCIAL HOUSE IN ORDER MAY NOT SOUND LIKE your idea of a bucket list item, it is the one thing I believe should be on everyone's bucket list because of the massive impact it has on your future and the future of your loved ones.

Many people start thinking about retirement in their thirties, but because developing a retirement plan requires a good deal of work, most don't do anything about it until much later. But the sooner you can begin, the more success you will have.

While there are plenty of books on financial planning that can help you get started, I always suggest working with a financial planner. The financial services industry can be dauntingly complex without expert guidance. As you'll be trusting this person with your money, be sure to do your homework in selecting your financial planner. One important question to ask is, "Are you legally required to act as a fiduciary?" A fiduciary is an advisor who must legally act in *your* best interest and *not theirs.* Knowing the answer to this question can make the difference between feeling confident in the plan you develop together or mistrusting the way your assets are handled.

Landing a Promotion or Ideal Job

N<small>AVIGATING THIS BUCKET LIST ITEM REQUIRES FIRST CONSIDERING</small> which of these two options is better for you. If you do not like the company you are working for, getting a promotion is not likely to change that. If you like the company but are simply bored with your present position, a lateral transfer to a different department could solve the problem.

If you're happy where you are and would like additional compensation for your efforts, a great first step is to get a copy of the job description for the position you want.

Knowing what is needed to excel in a new position allows you to hone your abilities in the required areas before making a move. When interviewing for the new position, you will be prepared to talk about how you have the skills required for the position.

While you are preparing yourself, you may also consider talking to your boss about your interest in a promotion. Not only will she or he likely be able to offer helpful suggestions on ways to prepare for the next level, you will also be top of mind when a position opens up.

If a promotion or transfer won't do the trick, and you know you want to get out and try something new, you may be ready to look for your ideal job. But leaving the place you know can be scary. You'll be starting anew, having to learn new procedures and prove yourself to new people.

If you're unsure about changing jobs or careers, look for volunteer openings in the area of work you are considering. For example, if you're considering becoming a nurse or x-ray technician, volunteering at a nearby hospital could give you a feel for the environment. Volunteering can be a rewarding and inexpensive way to try out a new job before making any big career changes.

Once you've chosen your direction, the same principles apply as before. Write down your goal, read it aloud twice daily, break down the steps required, and make a plan including a clear timeline. Then act on your plan!

SECTION TWO

THE NO-REGRET BUCKET LIST

The No-Regret Bucket List

A GOOD FRIEND OF MINE WORKED FOR THE SOCIAL SECURITY Department for many years and would tell me stories of people coming to apply for social security. So many of these people had stories of regret.

One man told my friend that when he was younger, he really wanted to be a commercial artist. But his wife insisted he go into the family clothing business to work with her father. He put aside his dreams and did as she wanted.

The man acknowledged the work had given them security and allowed him to make a good living, but he always regretted never pursuing his passion for art. By the time he shared his story with my friend, his sight was so bad he was unable to make his dream happen.

Another story my friend shared with me involved a very successful gentleman who owned his own business. As he filed for retirement benefits, he told my friend how he had poured his life into building the business, but as a result, he did not spend much time with his two sons as they were growing up. Now, both are married and have their own children, and they have little time to spend with their father outside their own families.

No matter the specifics, reaching your senior years carrying many regrets is a sad story. A bucket list is one way to proactively avoid that fate. Every item on your bucket list that you work towards and complete is one more achievement that will never end up on your regret list.

For that reason, I encourage you to think big. Allow your thoughts, expectations, and dreams to expand beyond anything you imagined before.

Don't just think about going skiing. Think about skiing the most exciting slopes you can imagine. Don't just think about hiking your local park. How about hiking the hills of Italy? Why restrict yourself to the pond around the corner when you could go boating on the Great Lakes or even the Mediterranean Sea?

Whatever you expect with conviction tends to come true, so use this knowledge to your advantage. If you expect small results, chances are you'll get small results. But if you expect the world, it's yours.

SECTION THREE

WHY TRAVEL?

The Travel Bucket List

WITH A WIDE WORLD OF PLACES TO EXPLORE, MANY BUCKET LISTS include some form of travel. There are plenty of reasons to chart your course to new places, but only you can decide how much travel is right for you. Consider the following motivations for travel, and see which apply to you and your dreams.

As you reflect, remember each example provided here may easily fit into multiple categories. For example, leisure travel might also include culinary adventures or be socially motivated. Mixing and matching travel motivations is highly encouraged!

Leisure Travel

WHEN MOST OF US THINK OF TAKING A TRIP, LEISURE TRAVEL IS THE first thing that comes to mind. It involves traveling to relax, have fun, and enjoy a change of pace from our usual daily routines. You may have always dreamed of going somewhere specific, or you may find yourself inspired by a friend's description of a recent vacation. The leisure travel category offers an endless array of possible bucket list items. The only limit is your imagination.

Culinary Travel

DO YOU LOVE COOKING? EXPLORING EXOTIC CUISINES? A KEEN INTEREST in food and its preparation can easily motivate your bucket list choices.

Travel your own country, or explore the world while sampling a wide variety of cuisines and flavors. Or, make a list of the dishes and cooking styles you'd like to learn, and seek out classes that cater to your list.

Religious Travel

RELIGIOUS TRAVEL OFFERS ANOTHER UNIQUE TWIST ON BUCKET LIST traveling. You can travel to beautiful cathedrals around the world, or broaden your horizons by visiting houses of worship of a variety of world religions. Whether you want to study religions more deeply, seek to pay homage to those who have gone before by visiting world-famous shrines, or just want to take in the sights, religious travel may be a fit for your bucket list.

Adventure Travel

IF YOU WANT TO EXPERIENCE THE FULL SPECTRUM OF WHAT THE WORLD has to offer, adventure traveling may be for you. For those who dream of the far reaches of the planet - visiting the Arctic Circle, seeing the Northern Lights, snorkeling the Great Barrier Reef, exploring the Galapagos Islands - bucket list adventures abound.

Cultural Travel

ADVENTURES TAKE ALL FORMS; RATHER THAN CONFRONTING NATURE'S extremes, learning the customs of another culture might be more your speed. If immersing yourself in a different culture, learning a new language, exploring a culture's art history, or even volunteering as a relief aid worker appeals to you, a cultural adventure could make an excellent bucket list item.

Fun Travel

Not every trip has to include panoramic landscapes or ancient monuments to feel momentous and life-changing. For some of us, fun is the top priority.

Do you love roller coasters? Maybe your bucket list could include riding on all the great roller coasters of the world. If you enjoy sharing crazy stories with your friends about your travels, a road trip full of unusual landmarks, such as the famous Wall of Gum in Seattle, Washington, might tickle your funny bone and give you tons of fun stories to tell.

Photo adventures are another excellent bucket list option. You can hunt wild game with your camera instead of a gun, capture rare birds or butterflies in flight, photograph the bridges of America, and so much more.

To up the adrenaline factor in your fun trip even further, there are companies out there that offer the opportunity to:

1. Drive a race car
2. Skydive
3. Fly a fighter jet plane

And so much more.

If you're looking for fun, it's easy to find. Simply focus on your goal, and look for all the opportunities around you.

Socially-Motivated Travel

IF YOU'VE EVER BEEN TO A FAMILY REUNION OR HAVE TAKEN A TRIP TO see the country where your ancestors were born, you're already familiar with socially-motivated travel. Events related to your family's history, first-time meetings with family you've never met before, weddings, and even graduation ceremonies are all excellent reasons to get out of your comfort zone and support the people you love by traveling.

Beyond family connections, socially-motivated travel can also include hobbyist conventions or trips, class reunions, alumni events, and meeting up with old friends.

Travel to Get Away

_____

SOMETIMES WE ALL NEED A BREAK, AND TRAVELING TO GET AWAY CAN BE just the change of pace we need. But since no two people's lives are alike, "getting away" can mean just about anything, leaving this category wide open for bucket list items.

Perhaps you feel a need to get away from the hustle and bustle of city life; a remote locale could feel like the perfect escape. Maybe life has been stressful, and you want to take a mental break by attending a silence retreat. No matter what "getting away" means to you, your escape will probably look very different from your regular life.

Dramatic escapes from the ordinary could include things like skydiving, white water rafting, spelunking, or retreating to a hut on remote Pacific island with no TV or cell phone. But it doesn't matter if your escape is dramatic or more low-key. There is no wrong way to get away.

Travel for Follow-Up on Education

Do you remember studying specific places, cities, or countries in school and dreaming of visiting them? Or maybe you had a chance to take a trip somewhere amazing, but it was many years ago. You always told yourself you'd go back again but never got around to it. A trip to learn something new or follow up on education started years before can be a fantastic addition to your bucket list.

Business Travel

MOST PEOPLE DO NOT ASSOCIATE BUSINESS TRAVEL AND BUCKET LISTS, but they should. While going on a business trip might not be at the top of your bucket list, with a little creativity and planning, that business trip could be your ticket to checking off another item on your bucket list in a timely, cost-effective way.

Let's say you have a business meeting in Orlando, Florida. If going to Disney World and Universal Studios happened to be on your list, you could extend your stay slightly to take advantage of your proximity. Or perhaps car races are more your style - Daytona Beach, home of the Daytona 500, is just up the coast. History buffs might opt to visit the oldest city in America, St. Augustine. And only an hour's drive from Orlando is NASA's launch facility at Cape Canaveral, which also easily warrants a visit. And the nearby Canaveral Cruise Port serves as a bustling departure point for beautiful, relaxing ocean cruises.

Even if these specific things aren't on your list, the point is there are many opportunities to weave your bucket list into your life. When traveling, for business or to any pre-planned occasion or event, remember to consider your list. See if any of your dreams happen to be close to your existing destination.

Getting Ready for Foreign Travel

DO YOU NEED A PASSPORT? DO YOU NEED A VISA? DO YOU NEED SHOTS? These are just a very few of what is sure to be a long list of questions you will have before leaving for another country. By planning ahead, you can learn what to expect, build excitement for the trip, and familiarize yourself with the culture before you go.

To help you prepare, you can:

- Check to see if there is an area of your city where there is a large population of people from the area you plan to visit. If there is, go there, stroll around, and stay long enough to eat dinner.
- If your city doesn't have a concentration of the population you will be visiting, look online. Some cities have social clubs or meetups for people from specific parts of the world.
- Talk to relatives, friends, and acquaintances who are familiar with the part of the world you are visiting.
- Look into the foreign embassies or consulates for the place(s) you are going. Many have individuals whose sole job is to promote tourism to their country. They are happy

to respond to phone calls, letters and email requests for information.

- Visit your local library or shop for books and videos on world travel.

SECTION FOUR

MODES OF TRAVEL

Modes of Travel

WHILE WORKING ON MY OWN BUCKET LIST, I HAVE ENCOUNTERED AND enjoyed many forms of travel. Some of these means of transportation were just that, but others were bucket list items themselves.

If you ever get to Sedona, Arizona, I suggest you take a Jeep tour. I took the Pink Jeep Tour twice and thoroughly enjoyed both experiences. We ventured into the rocky outback surrounding Sedona, where I learned Walt Disney used to take his artists for inspiration. The Painted Desert Ride at Disneyland, as well as the Nautilus submarine in Disney's "Twenty Thousand Leagues Under the Sea," were both inspired by rock formations from the area.

During a trip to Alaska, I visited a dog sled training camp and got to take a dog sled ride; another time, when I was in Hawaii, I took an actual submarine ride to the bottom of the ocean and watched beautiful fish and stingrays swim by. During the same trip, I also walked the rim of a live volcano. Many of my bucket list items have involved fun and unusual forms of transportation.

Your Selection of Travel Modes

As you think about your bucket list, you will want to take into account the various modes of travel that will help you achieve your goals. Common modes of travel include:

1. Driving
2. Flying
3. Cruises
4. Biking or walking
5. Train or bus

Each has its pros and cons.

Driving

JOURNEYING BY CAR ALLOWS YOU TO TRAVEL AT YOUR OWN PACE. YOU can take side trips along the way, an advantage that many other modes of travel do not offer, but driving has its disadvantages, too. A few good initial questions to consider include:

1. How long is the trip?
2. How many people are going?
3. What are the ages of the people going?
4. Can someone assist with the driving?

There is also the question of cost. Many people assume that driving will be less expensive than other modes of travel, but be sure to take a realistic look at the numbers before making your decision. Even a two-day car trip for two people quickly adds up: a one-night hotel stay, six meals apiece, and gas, not to mention the wear and tear on the vehicle.

Flying

FLYING IS OFTEN THE QUICKEST AND BEST WAY TO TRAVEL LONGER distances. It does require planning ahead, though: You'll need to take into account not only the ticket cost but also the round-trip drive to and from the airport, parking fees, baggage checking fees, and money for snacks and meals. Considering the Transportation Security Administration (TSA) recommendation to arrive at the airport two hours before your flight, you may discover alternate modes of travel a better fit for shorter trips within the 200-300 mile range.

Cruise

CRUISES ARE NOT FOR EVERYONE, BUT CRUISES ARE ONE OF THE FASTEST growing segments of the travel industry, and they provide an opportunity to complete several bucket list items at one time. Many cruises sail into several countries within a single trip, and there are unique bucket list experiences along the way. For example, on a cruise to Bermuda I took advantage of a coinciding nighttime sailing adventure into the mysterious Bermuda Triangle. It was an amazing trip that is still a great conversation starter today.

Cruises can be costly investments, but the price of a cruise includes meals and entertainment, which means less out-of-pocket spending during your trip. Don't forget the cost of a cruising also includes getting to the pier for departure, plus any parking fees. And you will want to take into account the additional cost of any shore excursions you might want to take.

Insider tip: If you plan to enjoy more than one cruise as part of your bucket list, check out the "future cruises" desk, available on most cruise ships. By taking advantage of incentives, discounts, and reduced deposits, you can get more out of your next cruise with perks like extra on-board credit. Many times, it is not even necessary to actually select dates for your next cruise: When you make the reduced deposit, you have up to two years to select and book your next adventure.

Train and Bus

TRAINS AND BUSES USUALLY TAKE MORE TRAVEL TIME THAN OTHER modes of travel, but both share the advantage of allowing the traveler to relax and enjoy the passing scenery.

Many companies offer multi-day train and bus tours to beautiful parts of the country, with plenty of fun stops along the way. Trips like these are usually a week or two long and often include a professional guide who is ready to share information and answer questions along the way. The traveler's job is to simply sit back and take it all in.

Walking or Cycling

FOR THOSE WHO ENJOY MORE ACTIVE TRAVEL, WALKING AND CYCLING tours are becoming quite popular. There are now several companies that provide both walking and cycling tours of places around the world.

Friends of mine recently took a walking tour of Italy, traveling from Florence to Rome, two cities on many people's bucket lists. Their trip was a combination adventure, activity, fun, and romance.

Summary of Travel Modes

THERE ARE MANY MODES OF TRAVEL; A MODE OF TRANSPORTATION might, itself, be an item on your bucket list. Your list might include taking your first airplane ride. It might include riding on an old steam-powered train. How can you make your journey to your bucket list destinations bucket list worthy, too?

I recently arranged a trip for clients of mine combining several modes of travel. They flew from Washington D.C. to Munich, Germany, then took a seven-day river cruise down the Danube River. The cruise ended in Budapest, Hungary. From there they took a train to Florence, Italy, where they embarked on a nine-day walking tour of Tuscany before heading back to the United States.

When considering a bucket list item, ask yourself if the method of travel could enhance the experience. If you want to take a cruise, can you combine it with your first train or plane ride on the way to the cruise departure point? Is driving a car the best way to see the scenery of a location, or would a domed rail car or a bus be a better option?

SECTION FIVE

TYPES OF BUCKET LISTS

Types of Bucket Lists

BUCKET LISTS COME IN ALL SHAPES AND SIZES, BUT THERE ARE A FEW common types that may work for you.

Individual

An individual bucket list is, as its name implies, a list put together by an individual and for that individual. Items on the list may involve other people, but the choice to include that item on the list was not theirs. The items on the list are personal to the individual writing the list.

Spouses or Partners

A LIST THAT TWO PEOPLE WILL SHARE MAY BE CONSTRUCTED individually or collaboratively. Each person could develop their own list to complete (like an individual list with added accountability from a partner who is also working on their list), or the couple may jointly develop a list.

Even when a couple decides to each have their own bucket list, completing each list while also preserving a happy relationship will require both parties to work together. For example, the couple might travel at the same time, but to different places. Or they might travel together to the same location but each complete different list items while there.

Then there is also the question of financing. Will bucket list costs come out of the family budget, or individual accounts or earnings? If there are children in the family, will the couple need to travel separately so one of them can be home with the kids?

Family Bucket List

A FAMILY BUCKET LIST IS NOT ONLY REALISTIC BUT CAN BE A WONDERFUL teaching tool. It is not a parent wishlist pushed on the children; it is a list built on input from everyone in the family. Creating a list like this takes time and patience but can serve as a wonderful tool to encourage communication among family members.

Children may have their own individual bucket lists, too. Oftentimes items on a bucket list will be age-related and thus will change over time. A child in elementary school might feel they cannot survive without a trip to Lego Land. High schoolers might find a trip to another state with the school band or debate club a must. For college students, a bucket list item might be a semester abroad or renting a house with friends over spring break. Once they graduate, if they have been encouraged to maintain their own bucket list, children are more likely to stay with the process. When started early, a bucket list and its continual growth and expansion can become a lifelong joy.

For family lists as well as children's bucket lists, the parents' job is to keep the planning realistic. This dose of reality is not intended to repress the creativity or imagination but rather to channel it. With supportive guidance, a child's list could contain items designed to support and further education, such as exploring the cultures of various countries by way of Disney's Epcot Center.

Generational Bucket List

TODAY, MULTIPLE GENERATIONS OF FAMILIES MAY ALL LIVE TOGETHER. Specifically, many families now include not only parents and children but also grandparents, aunts, uncles, cousins, and even close family friends who spend significant time together.

If your family is expansive or multi-generational, consider including everyone as you create your family bucket list. Perhaps, as a family, you would like to spend more time traveling and visiting with family members in other states. Family reunions, reuniting with an individual family member, and conducting genealogical research would all be ways to achieve this goal.

Which type of bucket list is right for you?

SECTION SIX

MAKING THE LIST

IF YOU HAVE NOT ALREADY WRITTEN DOWN A LIST OF THINGS YOU WANT to do, see, and achieve in your lifetime, it is time to construct your list.

When you first put pen to paper, let all your ideas flow out. Try not to edit or prioritize as you write; that will come later. Think big, but don't forget the little things. Skiing the Alps is a wonderful goal, but so is eating out at a fine restaurant once a month. It is just a question of what you want.

Your list may be very long. It may contain travel destinations, educational goals or ambitions, "firsts" (such as first airplane trip or first time ziplining), "all of a kind" (visiting the homes of all the US presidents, or watching a game in every major league ballpark), natural wonders, adventure, and so much more.

You may also have personal goals, like spending more time with the family. No matter what it is, if you want to do it, put it on the list.

Refining the List

ONCE YOU HAVE YOUR UNRESTRICTED LIST, IT IS TIME TO SHRINK IT down to a workable number of items. This can be done by applying filters and reality checks.

Most of us face a few limiting factors that need to be considered when constructing a bucket list. For example, if you are sixty years old and want to spend each Christmas in a different U.S. state, you will need luck on your side to complete it - you'll need to live past 110. Likewise, if you want to run the fastest mile but have an artificial leg, your parameters for success may need to change. Maybe you want to spend two months a year on a private island accessible only by private plane, but you only make minimum wage at your current job. These goals are not impossible, but they are unrealistic given your current circumstances. You might want to refine your goal to be a better fit, or you might choose to prioritize another goal first.

Filters to Consider

COMMON RESTRICTIONS OR FILTERS TO CONSIDER INCLUDE:

1. Number of items on the list
2. Time commitments
3. Safety
4. Physical ability or condition
5. Cost
6. Overlapping bucket list items

In addition to these filters, you may choose to impose additional restrictions based on your personal situation. If you use a wheelchair or walker, have specific dietary needs, require special sight and hearing accommodations, you should consider your needs in your planning.

Let's take a closer look at our common filters.

Number of Items

WHILE YOUR UNFILTERED BUCKET LIST MAY BE QUITE LONG, YOUR finalized bucket list should be filtered down to a realistic number of items. You want your list to feel doable and exciting, not impossible and overwhelming.

There is no prescription for the "right" number of items; your final number will depend on your personal circumstances and desires as well as the location and nature of your listed items.

To guide the process, I often suggest to my clients to filter and sort their unfiltered list down as much as possible, then review the list and choose six items to start with.

I ask them to select:

1. Three short-term items that can be completed in two years or less
2. Two mid-term items to complete in the next four years
3. One long-term goal you will complete in the next six years

These six items become your priority bucket list.

Prioritizing in this way is important because it provides a timeline and structure, giving you direction and focus. It establishes the order in which you will accomplish the overall list.

As you accomplish your short-term items, your mid-range items will become your new short-term goals. Each time you cross a bucket list item off your list, you have the opportunity to revisit your master list and add new, long-range items to your priority list.

Time Commitments

HOW MUCH TIME WILL IT TAKE TO ACHIEVE YOUR GOAL? SOME PEOPLE have great flexibility with their schedules; others operate on strict time tables. Clearly if you are working, you have less time than if you are retired. The amount of time you have available verses the time it will take to complete your list items can be a powerful filter in helping you prioritize.

As you review your list, here are some questions to ask yourself:

1. How much time will each bucket list item take? Do you need a two-week trip, or can you complete your goal over a long weekend?
2. If an item on your list will take a long time to complete, is it possible to break it into smaller segments?
3. How much vacation do you get at work? How much notice do you need to give to get time off? Does your company allow you to accumulate vacation time?
4. Are others joining you? Do you need to coordinate schedules with others before moving forward?

Safety

IT IS IMPORTANT TO UNDERSTAND THE RISKS OF ANY ADVENTURE THAT takes you outside of your comfort zone. The more prepared you are, the more safely and enjoyably you can cross items off your list.

Ask yourself the following questions to evaluate the safety of the items on your list:

1. If you are going to a different country, what is the degree of political unrest in that country?
2. What is the local crime situation where you are headed? Is there any possible threat of terrorist activity?
3. Are there any local diseases or other health issues you should know about?
4. What medical facilities are available at your destination?
5. Will you be in an extreme climate? Elevation, temperature, and UV strength can pose health concerns no matter what country you're in.

If you are traveling to a remote or lightly populated area, engaging the services of a reputable local guide can add an element of safety to your trip.

Your Physical Health

MANY PEOPLE HAVE PERSONAL HEALTH ISSUES THAT AFFECT THE selection of items on their list. Arthritis, high blood pressure, knee or ankle problems, and even allergies can quickly filter down a long list of possible bucket list items.

Preparation can help with many of these challenges. Consider the following questions:

1. Do you have a health condition that could impact how you travel? For example, those with heart or lung issues may not be able to fly.
2. If you take prescription drugs, will your supply last for the length of your trip? Do you need any refills or new prescriptions before you go?
3. Are there medical supplies you should take with you in case of emergency? If you know you have knee problems, you might want to pack your knee brace. If you're camping in the outback, an extensive first-aid kit would be good to bring.
4. Do you have concerns about your physical well-being during your trip? If so, schedule a checkup with your doctor ahead of time.

Cost

FOR MOST PEOPLE, COST IS A FILTER FOR EVERY ITEM ON THEIR BUCKET
list. But it doesn't have to be a dealbreaker. Some bucket list items can
be paid for over time. You might save up money for others. They key
is to be realistic.

If you earn $50,000 a year, have a family, and sometimes struggle
just to cover normal expenses, a $200,000 trip, while not impossible
to save for, would be very difficult at best.

When you have a costly item on your list, try breaking expensive
bucket list items into smaller sub-goals or segments. As the saying
goes, "How do you eat an elephant?" The answer is, "One bite at a
time."

Careful consideration of all the various costs of a trip can be
helpful as well. Think about the following expenses when budgeting
for your trip:

Air travel:

*Ticket price, baggage fees, gas or taxi fare to get to the airport, parking
fees, meals, and possibly lodging between flights, depending on your
itinerary.*

Driving:

Gas, hotels, meals, parking fees.

Cruise:

Price of the cruise, getting to the pier (gas or airfare), pre-cruise meals, parking fees, lodging before the cruise departs, plus the cost of any purchases or shore excursions you might take.

Train or bus:

Ticket price, getting to the station, parking fees, meals, any side excursions along the way.

Walking or cycling:

Appropriate clothing and shoes, bike rental or purchase and repair, meals, lodging, possible gym membership to prepare physically.

Overlapping Lists

When couples or families include individuals who are each working on their own list, there will come a time to compare lists. Reviewing and combining your lists can be an excellent way to filter down your items.

When you are ready to do so, the first step is to see if the lists contain any identical or overlapping items. The second step is to see if any non-overlapping items can be adjoined or combined into a single trip that meets everyone's goals.

For example, if one person wanted to see Monticello, Thomas Jefferson's Charlottesville, Virginia estate, and the other person wished to visit all the homes of America's presidents, one goal could be crossed off for itself while also supporting the other goal. Furthermore, Virginia is an excellent place to visit presidential homes: Eight presidents were born on her soil, more than any other state, so additional forays to other nearby presidential homes could be added into the trip.

Similarly, if one person wants to see a landmark that is located in an area the other person wants to visit during a specific season (fall foliage for example), the two trips could be combined into one.

Looking for similar items across your respective lists or items in adjoining geographic locations can help you identify high-priority places and focus your bucket list efforts.

SECTION SEVEN

PLANNING AHEAD

Developing the Plan

Now it is time to develop a plan to accomplish the items on your prioritized "top six" bucket list.

The best person to help you with your plan will be your travel agent. If you don't have one, get one. It will be well worth it in terms of time, effort, and cost.

Using a travel agent to guide your bucket list efforts is a good idea for many reasons. A few of them include:

1. **Smooth travels:** Most bucket lists include some form of travel. A travel agent has professional knowledge and expertise in travel to ensure your trips go as smoothly as possible. They know which locations require a passport versus a visa and how to navigate the system and requirements so you can confidently carry the right documents for your trip.

2. **Cost:** They know which hotels have price deals, who is currently offering promotions, and how to take advantage of packages. With the help of an agent, you might be able to combine two or three things on your list into a single trip, saving you time, money, and frustration and allowing you to achieve more in less time.

3. **Lodging and comfort:** Travel agents know when the weather is best in your intended destination, and they can tell you which hotels are new, which have been recently refurbished, and which ones to avoid.
4. **Safety:** They know which places are experiencing unrest and should be avoided by travelers.
5. **Activities:** They know which cruises and resorts offer which tours and excursions and which countries or locations have heavy tourist restrictions.
6. **Currency:** Travel agents can look up and explain currency exchange rates in the places you want to travel, and they can help you prepare or even exchange money before you go.
7. **Access:** Thanks to their connections and industry knowledge, a good travel agent can find information about any place you are traveling more quickly and easily than you can.

No matter where you are going, it is safe to assume a travel agent will be able to help you arrange efficient and cost-effective travel. But what about bucket list items that do not involve travel?

Even for non-travel items, your travel agent can help. Most agents have a wide variety of clients, and they participate in networking groups, business organizations, and civic groups. Thanks to their connections, there is a very good chance your agent will know just the person to help you, no matter what you are planning. For example, if you want to take dance lessons but don't know where to start, your agent may have a dance instructor as a client, or they may know someone who took lessons in preparation for their wedding.

Sharing Your List

BECAUSE OF HIS OR HER EXPERIENCE, CONNECTIONS, AND EXPERTISE, your travel agent is an excellent person to ask to review your bucket list. Your travel agent can serve as an impartial third party ready to support you.

If it is an individual list, you should also discuss your list with your spouse, children, and any other family members living with you since they will likely be affected by the list.

Beyond those who will be immediately impacted, be cautious with whom you openly share your list. Though you may be ecstatic over your upcoming adventures, friends and non-immediate relatives may not share your dreams. They may be quick to label the items on your or your family's list as silly, too expensive, too large, or simply unreasonable. But it is really your opinion that counts. Remember, only the people who create a bucket list have the right to decide if an item is unreasonable or not.

Staying Flexible

ALTHOUGH YOU WILL END UP SPENDING A FAIR AMOUNT OF TIME developing your list, never think of it as set in stone. Remember, life happens. A change in health, income, or time commitments might mean you need to change up your priority order or even revise or replace specific items on the list.

No matter what you want to do, see, or accomplish, remember you can do so at your own pace. My recommended time frames for bucket list items are suggestions only. You might discover you are more comfortable with a different schedule based on your list and your personal goals.

Annual Review

WHAT SEEMS IMPORTANT TODAY MAY NOT BE SO IMPORTANT TOMORROW. Both your unfiltered master bucket list and your filtered six-item list should be reviewed annually. I suggest scheduling the review ahead of time (or it may not get done). During this review, items accomplished should be checked off, existing items should be reconsidered and possibly rearranged, and new items should be added to the priority list to replace those that have been completed.

SECTION EIGHT

PROTECTING YOUR INVESTMENT

Protecting Your Investment

IF YOU ARE INVESTING IN YOURSELF BY TRAVELING AND FOLLOWING YOUR bucket list dreams, I strongly recommend protecting any travel investment over five hundred dollars with travel insurance.

When my clients turn down travel insurance, I have them sign the following statement: *"I decline the offer to protect my investment."*

While the purpose of this statement is partially to protect me from a lawsuit if something goes awry, it also serves to emphasize the seriousness of the decision to forego insurance.

The Real Costs of Insurance

THERE ARE TWO REASONS I AM SO PASSIONATE ABOUT TRAVEL insurance. The first reason is because it is not costly to include in trip planning (especially compared with the investment you are making in the trip itself) and gives you great flexibility in case things do not go as planned. With travel insurance for your trip, you can cancel and reschedule your trip due to personal health reasons, unexpected scheduling problems, unrest in the country you're visiting, or issues or conflicts that arise for your traveling companions.

Airlines and cruise lines may offer trip cancellation insurance (though some cancellation credits may only be reimbursed in the form of future travel vouchers), but many companies now offer more comprehensive travel insurance. These plans often cover lost luggage, cancelled flights, and sometimes even provide life insurance.

While travel insurance like this could be considered expensive because it is only in effect for a short period of time, there are many things that can go very badly while traveling. Even one thing going awry makes the insurance worth the investment. One of the most expensive items that can be covered by travel insurance is medical transportation back to your country of origin, known as expatriation coverage. If while traveling abroad you become gravely ill, and you need to be airlifted back home for treatment, it is a huge expense and definitely worth the cost of insurance.

Even in less extreme scenarios, such as losing your luggage, travel insurance can cover the unexpected out-of-pocket expenses to replace everything. Thanks to insurance, those costs will be reimbursed, often within a day or two.

The second reason I am a staunch advocate of travel insurance is because of the number of travel stories I have seen and heard. Here are just a few examples.

Years ago, I was on a cruise when one of the passengers suffered a heart attack. The ship's doctor did not have equipment on board to perform open heart surgery; the passenger needed a hospital as soon as possible. Rather than sail into the Gulf of Mexico as originally planned, the ship diverted, heading for Florida. A hospital helicopter was sent from land to the ship, and the passenger was airlifted to the hospital. A helicopter airlift costs thousands. Though I didn't know the man, I was concerned not only for his health but for his wallet. I hoped he had travel insurance to cover the costs.

On another cruise I took with my wife and stepson, my stepson's luggage was delivered to his cabin badly damaged. Since I always get travel insurance, within two days a check was issued through the ship's customer service representative. Thanks to insurance, we were able to purchase new luggage to use for the rest of the trip.

Lastly, a fellow agent once told me a story of a man who took a helicopter from his home in Orange County, California to Disney Land, a distance of just twenty miles. The helicopter crashed after about ten miles of travel, and the man was killed. His travel insurance policy paid a death benefit of about twenty thousand dollars.

SECTION NINE

WHY A BUCKET LIST?

Let's Recap

WE'VE COVERED NUMEROUS REASONS AS TO WHY IT IS WORTH THE TIME, effort, and energy to create and pursue a bucket list. Let's review.

Firstly, there is the initial step of writing down all your ideas and dreams. Doing so expands your mind, encourages you to think of new possibilities, and gives you a starting place.

Secondly, there is the process of refining your list to reveal your current top priorities. This shorter list helps to prevent procrastination and allows you to focus on how to accomplish specific items on the list rather than feeling overwhelmed by the longer, unfiltered list. It ensures you have a plan to achieve goals that might otherwise become regrets.

The final step is to get going. Take action on your plan, and work with a travel agent to take advantage of the best possible timing and pricing options for your dreams.

Be Ready for Inspiration

DO NOT BE SURPRISED IF, WHILE ENJOYING ONE ITEM ON YOUR LIST, YOU discover there is more to see, learn, and do than you imagined. You may end up adding items to your bucket list, or you may even find yourself led in an unexpected direction.

My niece and her husband went to Harpers Ferry in Maryland for a long weekend of relaxing. They were not working on a bucket list. As a matter of fact, they did not even have a bucket list. But while they were there, they decided to take an evening ghost tour. Their guide wove spine-chilling stories into the history of the town with such skill they decided to seek out ghost stories in other towns and states, too. Without intending to, they went from no bucket list to one that will keep them busy for quite a while.

Similarly, three years ago, some friends of mine decided they wanted to do something different for Christmas. Their children were grown and no longer celebrated with them the traditional ways, so rather than sitting at home staring at decorations, they decided it was time to take their first cruise. They enjoyed it so much it immediately became an annual event. Now they look forward to taking a cruise to a different country each year.

Here's another example of getting creative with your bucket list. As mentioned before, Virginia is the "Mother of Presidents" with eight US presidents born on her soil (George Washington, Thomas Jefferson, James Madison, James Monroe, William Harrison, John Taylor, Zachary Taylor, and Woodrow Wilson all still have property honoring them in their home state). If your goal were to visit the homes of all the US presidents, a two-week Virginia vacation could get you almost twenty percent of the way to your goal. The homes of Jefferson, Madison and Monroe are all within twenty-eight miles of each other.

Not only could you cross off a substantial number of presidential homes quite quickly, visiting any one of these properties could pique a new interest or even send you in a whole new direction.

For example, Washington was America's first president. While visiting his Mount Vernon home, you might learn that he led American troops in putting down the whisky rebellion. But he also ran a commercial distillery that, in 1799, produced almost 11,000 gallons of whiskey. This interesting fact might incite you to find out what the whiskey rebellion was about or to learn more about Washington's distillery. Did he ship outside of Virginia? Were there competitive distilleries nearby? Where or how did he get his supplies for making whiskey? You can see how quickly one bucket list item can expand into multiple new interests.

Similarly, Jefferson was America's first Secretary of State, but during his term of office, he resigned from George Washington's cabinet. If you're into history, you might want to dig deeper to find out why he made that choice. Likewise, Jefferson was one of five members of the Continental Congress selected to write a document declaring American independence from Great Britain. You might want to find out who the other four members were and learn more about them as individuals, especially since they decided Jefferson should be the one to write the declaration. Who were they, and why did they make that choice?

Keep Your Eyes Open

REMEMBER YOUR BUCKET LIST CAN GROW AND EVOLVE AT ANY POINT. Pay attention to your reaction to what is shared on the news, the things you read about in books, and even the natural events happening around the world.

For example, the eruption of Mount Saint Helens might lead to a visit to the eruption site or spur on an interest in visiting other active volcano sites. There are one hundred and sixty-nine active volcanoes in the United States alone (fifty-five of them are considered serious threats), so this interest could keep you busy for a while.

SECTION TEN

ITEMS FOR THE LIST

Types of Items for the List

YOUR BUCKET LIST SHOULD BE UNIQUELY YOURS, BUT THE FOLLOWING list of possible bucket list items is provided with the hope that it inspires ideas for your list. Feel free to circle, annotate, number, prioritize, or otherwise mark up this section with your own notes.

I encourage you to consider, then comment, on each item listed below, even if your comment is, "That's stupid - I would never do it." Both positive and negative reactions to the types of items listed here can help you decide which items or types of items should be on your own personal list.

Bucket List Items for Education

- go back to school to earn a specific degree
- learn to SCUBA dive
- learn to skydive or fly a plane
- learn to knit, sew, dance, paint, rock climb, etc. *(any new hobby offers a learning opportunity!)*
- take music lessons
- see how Christmas celebrations differ state to state or country to country

"First Time" Bucket List Items

- first train ride
- first zipline
- first airplane flight
- first time leaving the country

"All of a Kind" Bucket List Items

- visit all 50 states
- set foot on all the continents of the world
- visit all the major league baseball stadiums
- see all the US National Monuments *(Mount Rushmore, the Saint Louis Arch, the Washington Monument, etc.)*
- visit all the US presidential homes

Natural Wonders Bucket List Items

- the Grand Canyon
- the Great Barrier Reef
- the Alps
- the great rivers of the world
- Glacier National Park
- the great waterfalls of the world
- Arizona's red rock formations
- Monument Valley (Utah)
- the Aurora Borealis

Adventure Bucket List Items

- fly a jet plane
- skydive
- drive a race car
- climb frozen waterfalls
- swim with sharks
- motorcycle motocross
- white water rafting

It All Comes Down to This

PLANNING + ACTION = JOY AND ADVENTURE!

SECTION ELEVEN

REFERENCE INFORMATION

Major United States Airport Symbols

HERE ARE THE MAJOR UNITED STATES AIRPORT SYMBOLS:

Mobil Municipal Airport	MOB	Alabama
Montgomery Dannely Field	MGM	Alabama
Anchorage International	ANC	Alaska
Fairbanks International	FAI	Alaska
Phoenix Sky Harbor	PHX	Arizona
Tucson International	TUS	Arizona
Little Rock Regional	LIT	Arkansas
Los Angeles international	LAX	California
Sacramento Metropolitan	SMF	California
San Francisco International	SFO	California
Denver International	DEN	Colorado
Hartford Bradley Int'l	BDL	Connecticut
New Haven	HVN	Connecticut
Fort Lauderdale	FLL	Florida
Orlando Int'l	MCO	Florida
Miami Int'l	MIA	Florida
Tampa Int'l	TPA	Florida
Atlanta Int'l	ATL	Georgia
Honolulu Int'l	HNL	Hawaii
Boise Gowen Field	BOI	Idaho
Sun Valley	SUN	Idaho
Midway Int'l	MDA	Illinois
O' Hare Int'l	ORD	Illinois
Indianapolis Int'l	IND	Indiana
Des Moines Int'l	DSM	Iowa
Topeka Philip Billard	TOP	Kansas
Lexington Blue Grass	LEX	Kentucky
Louisville	SDF	Kentucky
Portland Int'l	PWN	Maine

Baltimore/ Washington	BWI	Maryland
Boston Logan Int'l	BOS	Massachusetts
Detroit City	DTW	Michigan
Minneapolis/St. Paul	MSP	Minnesota
Jackson	JAN	Mississippi
Billings	BIL	Montana
Kansas City Int'l	MCI	Missouri
Lincoln Municipal	LNK	Nebraska
Las Vegas	LAS	Nevada
Reno/Tahoe	RNO	Nevada
Concord	CON	New Hampshire
Atlantic City	ACY	New Jersey
Newark	EWR	New Jersey
Albuquerque	ABQ	New Mexico
Santa Fe	SAF	New Mexico
La Guardia	LGA	New York
Kennedy Int'l	JFK	New York
Douglas	CCLT	North Carolina
Hector Field	FAR	North Dakota
Bismarck Municipal	BIS	North Dakota
Cincinnati Int'l	CVG	Ohio
Cleveland	CLE	Ohio
Will Rogers Airport	OKC	Oklahoma
Eugene Airport	EUG	Oregon
Portland Airport	PDX	Oregon
Philadelphia Airport	PHL	Pennsylvania
Pittsburgh Int'l	PIT	Pennsylvania
Theodore F Green	PVD	Rhode Island
Charleston AFB Airport	CHS	South Carolina
Pierre Airport	PIR	North Dakota
Lovell Field	CHA	Tennessee
Memphis Int'l	MEM	Tennessee
Nashville Metro. Airport	MEM	Tennessee
Love Field	DAL	Texas
Fort Worth Int'l	DFW	Texas
George Bush Airport	IAH	Texas
San Antonio Int'l	SAT	Texas
Salt Lake City Int'l	SLC	Utah
Edward F Knapp	MPV	Vermont
Richmond Int'l Airport	RIC	Virginia
Norfolk Int'l Airport	ORF	Virginia
Seattle/Tacoma	SEA	Washington
Dulles Int'l Airport	IAD	Washington D.C.
Ronald Reagan	DCA	Washington D.C.
Yeager Airport	CRW	West Virginia
Austin Straubel Field	GRB	Wisconsin
General Mitchell Field	MKE	Wisconsin
Cheyenne Airport	CYS	Wyoming
Jackson Hole Airport	JAC	Wyoming

Major United States Air Carrier Phone Numbers and Websites

Here are the Major United States Air Carrier Phone Numbers and websites:

Aeromexico	800-237-6639	aeromexico.com
Air Canada	888-247-2262	aircanada.com
Alaska	800-252-7522	alaskaair.com
American	800-433-7300	aa.com.
British Airways	800-247-9297	britishairways.com
Delta	800-221-1212	delta.com
Jet Blue	800-538-2583	jetblue.com
Lufthansa	800-645-3880	lufthansa.com
South West	800-435-9792	southwest.com
Spirit	801-401-2222	spiritair.com
United	800-241-6522	united.com

Acknowledgments

The author wishes to thank these contributors:

Crystal Cregge – Illustrator

Crystal Cregge is a Graphic Designer, Illustrator, and Animator. She grew up with dreams of being a comic book artist but found her love of telling stories through imagery could be expressed in many mediums. Her work has ranged from children's books, audiobooks, commercials, TV shows, and magazines to postcards and even virtual reality. Crystal has a Bachelor's of Fine Arts from Virginia Commonwealth University.

Ali Johnson – Photographer

Ali Johnson is a nationally published portrait photographer locate near Charlottesville, Virginia. Ali has been married for 25 years and has two boys age 22 and 24. She loves shopping thrift stores and her studio is filled with her treasures that are often used in her photo sessions. She wants to photograph what makes you, you!Glamorous, happy-go-lucky, country, athletic. During your photo sessions, she wants to capture your unique personality. She says that your session should be a blast! If you aren't laughing and having fun, she has not done her job.

Kim Eley – Publishing Consultant

Kim Eley, CEO of KWE Publishing, is an author, a writing coach, a publishing consultant, and a speaker! She specializes in personal development books with practical takeaways where people share their real-life stories, and also in thoughtful children's books. The common thread of both is to help people see what's possible and shift to a more enjoyable, fulfilled life. She is the author of the book "Tickers: What Makes People....Tick! And Pursue a Career They Love!" Kim has a Bachelor's of Arts from the College of William & Mary and a Master of Arts from Virginia Commonwealth University. She adores cats, orchids, Marvel movies, cooking for her husband and friends, '80's hair metal, and gets all her news from comedy channels.

CPSIA information can be obtained
at www.ICGtesting.com
Printed in the USA
FSHW020412241121
86321FS